Bones We Made Together

Elizabeth Woods-Darby

Bones We Made Together
© 2026 Elizabeth Woods-Darby
ISBN: 9781966337317
Library of Congress Number: 2026901208
Cover art:
© 2025 Elizabeth Woods-Darby

First Edition, © 2026

Printed in the United States of America

Edited by Alana Benson
Cover Design by Sage Herrin
Layout Design by Jessica S. Lin

This book is dedicated to mothers:

doing the big, messy, invisible, excruciating and beautiful

work of loving and raising the world.

And for my mom Lucy,

from whom I learned how to love big

and how to big brave.

Bones

I am building my poems

a body.

So that they,

and I,

may run

free.

Table of Contents

Epilogue

Preface

Writing this book saved my life, giving me a chance to give voice to the world-changing heartbreak of 2020 through the lens of a brand-new mom..

Bones We Made Together was born one night in late 2020 while I was listening to Podrig O'Touma's podcast Poetry Unbound, elbow deep in fuchsia rubber gloves scrubbing shit stains off my family's toilet bowl. The poem of the episode was "One Tree" by Philip Metres (go listen to it), and I had to stop scrubbing because I was crying so hard.

It's a simple poem about neighbors arguing over a tree which shades both of their yards, but within its simple specificity, it somehow gave me the radical permission that I hadn't known I was asking for—for my story to matter and for this book to be born.

I wrote most of this book in a postpartum haze in the dark, sitting on the edge of my tub in our ancient bathroom and under blankets before sleep claimed me.

Looking back now, I know I was writing as a way to make the invisibility of my life appear somewhere, matter; for all my thoughts about our wild, beautiful and burning world to have a place where they belong.

Even before I became a parent, I had never been able to read a headline about a shooting and not think about who taught the gunman how to tie their shoes. Who clapped for their first steps. All these tiny invisible moments of love or silence, of sacrifice, meals and bedtime stories; the mute passing down of what was handed to us. I think about the quiet, excruciating — or heart blown-wide — kind of impacts these things have on our world.

Once I stepped through the portal of birth, the world shifted for me, deepening in its anguish and its beauty. As though I had shed layers that had kept me from the truth of myself, from seeing the truth of the world; from viscerally knowing how fleeting and tender and transient this life is.

Trying to hold a moment still is like trying to hold on to river water. It's made to keep going, keep flowing. These pages are marked with all the waterstains from my cupped hands as I tried not to miss it, or drown.

I hope, the way most parents hope for their kids to live their lives fully expressed, that this book gets to live fully in your life, expanding its meanings and metaphors into places I'll never see or taste or touch, but that you will.

May this book be a love letter for you, wherever you are. Full of grief and love, awe, anger and understanding, it is the labor of becoming a self; my self in a newer, deeper, more raw, unpracticed and authentic form.

I hope in some way it gives you permission to delve into the unexplored or undiluted parts of yourself too. And to know that wherever you are in your life's journey, you are not alone.

-Elizabeth Woods-Darby

Trigger warnings: In this book there are mentions of mom-truama and mom-specific abandonment. As well as murder, suicide, postpartum depression, gun-violence, miscarriage and cancer.

Please take care of yourself as you read.

EMDR therapy changed my life and greatly impacted my ability to write this book. If you are struggling with things in your life, consider this a nudge to find someone who can support you. No one needs to heal alone.

Bones We Made Together

DAXSON PUBLISHING

For Ellis:

Can you remember lifetimes in a single second?
Reach back into the star dark past, and touch

our history
heavy and sweet like ripe peaches in my summer hands / feel

a thousand road-trips we have already yet to take,
down roads too beautiful, too big, to mention, windows

down, music blaring, comfortable in the ruckus of it all together /

I'm only 7 weeks in.

/ so how can I know
what it feels like to be singing with you? Our voices

a remembering, even though inside of me
my body has yet to forge you a voice box

that you will one day
use joyously, flagrantly, hopefully, with your whole heart.

There was chaos before this,
before knowing you.

The face of your father overwhelmed
and unsteady on his feet as we leaned over the pee stick to peer
into our future with its two pink lines.

My heart stretches thin, feeling you waver, question
if you should come.
If you will be wanted.

I know now,   *I   want   you.*

Spine straightening,
ribs waxing to make more room
for growing the moon of you
and here you are,

rising,
alighting yourself like gold
in the warm dark
waters of my womb.

You are / *here*, you have landed—
you are riding in this boat of my belly,
sea of my blood
around you, my body is already busy

building you bones
stringing you nerves
muscles and skin.
A symphony being written and played at the same time.

I close my eyes, palm over where you are
 in my belly and time flattens out / fast forwarding in blinks

/ your birth-wet baby skin
on my bare chest /

/ then you are two, on the window seat upstairs
turning to me with all the wonder

of the world alive in your eyes and you tell me
"Mama, I love you!" /

/ your fingers reflexively reaching for me;
my hair, my skin, my hands —

holding — *both of us, holding on to the*
miracle of this / of each other.

Spring

The Battlefield

I think about the children
soldiers, wounded on the battlefield
the ones who
as the pain sears them
want their mothers

and I think about their mothers;
hundreds, sometimes, thousands
of miles away, pausing in the line at the grocery store
a hand to their constricted chest
suddenly unable to breathe.

The year I became a mother the world shuttered herself
against a global pandemic.
We stayed inside our houses
like the pits inside of stone fruit.
Maybe that's why my peach of a son

waited an extra two weeks
inside my body
my bones a stronghold, my muscles
rocking him back and forth to the tune of
not yet.

Not quite, yet.

I remember everyone in the delivery room
but just their eyes,
their soft, practiced, practical hands
guiding me closer to the edges
of myself;
forty-one hours in the dark waters of labor,
my blurry mind helpless
my body giving everything / anything
as we rode the 50 foot waves
one / after / another

their all consuming power
engulfing my body
until I became the striking point
between the unforgiving surge
of the sea and the towering rocks,
slippery at the shore.

I pushed   strained   stretched
stretching myself so thin you could see
the light
through me

and when I finally tore open,
and my son was born,
I too, arrived into this world
a new configuration
of woman.

The outside world felt unfathomably far away then.
As if there was a lamp turned on over us
and the rest of the world
was left out in complete darkness to me.

Though the birth had broken me,
I couldn't wait to return home,
my mother —who had known in her bones
I was pregnant before I even did—
standing in our doorway with her wide open arms.

She had come
to help me cross the bridge into Motherhood.
One capable arm around my waist,
her unshakable love held up like a light
to help show me the way across the postpartum water.

She was the first to hold him.
Her very first grandchild.

I watched her looking down at him;
love so ablaze it was like watching the warmth
of the sun rise in her face,
touching so gently
his tiny soft fists.

But it was as though something

m a s s i v e

gave way
under the heat
of that rising sun
inside of her then too.

A giant glacier, calving.

An ice cap cracking,   crumbling,   shattering
moved by the undeniable
power
of warming water.

That ancient ice-blue underbelly
a heart,
long lived in the arctic, untouched waters
was suddenly

Roaring.

Free.

Flipped face up to the sun.

The next morning, I awoke to my mom's frost-white
Prius waiting patiently in our driveway
tailgate open, her suitcase closed,
waiting for her by the door.

No explanation. A quick hug.
And she started her silent engine
and drove quietly away.

As if standing too close
to this love
would somehow break her
or burn her
in a way she could not afford.

I did not understand.

I couldn't walk yet by myself.
The birth had damaged my legs,
so I sat, trembling in my rocking chair,
cradling my days old son against my skin,
crying together.

Baptized in the salt of our own tears.

//

Becoming a Mother has been like being drafted into battle.

Each morning, I dutifully put on my uniform,
tie my hair back with a rubber band,
and nurse my child after another night of no sleep.

My heart / breath
throbbing like a wild bird
caught
in the confines of my throat / cage.

I am in the feral waters of motherhood
in the middle of this pandemic, and I am alone.

Trying to keep my son's head above the water. My throat

spluttering as the ink black waves hit my face
hoping to God
please,   please,   don't let us drown.

I am a soldier forgotten on a black-water battlefield.

I close my eyes and breathe,
listening for the breaks between the bullet rounds.
I missed the boat for basic training.
But I watch the smoke in the sky anyway,
waiting for when it's safe to hide and when to run
and when to stop and press my shaking hands
to the girlish blood pouring out of these fresh old wounds.

Did she feel me then?
Alive and dying
out here in the field?

I don't think so.

She went on buying her crackers and milk
behind her mask.
Her own fear like a blanket or a shield
keeping her safe and separate from me.

I have had to teach myself
how to walk again.
How to hold my son with my tender, raw, real self
so he knows in his bones
that he is loved.

I've had to learn to comfort my own bleeding body,
bleary, burning eyes in the bathroom mirror
whispering the words over and over again

I. can. do. this.

I can do this.

I   can   do   this

Maybe all mothers can feel this.
Maybe this is the feeling that doesn't go away
like clutching at the breath in my own chest
as if I could give it to my own child, make them breathe.

Even from a thousand miles away.

Broken Open

There is a rib cage floating above me.
A whole body of bones

made up of white cirrus clouds— a shoulder
drifts here, a tibia there; hips and a pelvis waiting

for their *inevitable* connection

I watch, like a broken bird from the ground—with my feet
that won't walk— my heart, a slivered field of safety glass.

Above me this body of clouds becomes something
new again; something strong

I ache to be.Though my bird body still thrums dully, still pumps
blue-red blood, still makes milk and weeps.

My eyes are locked above me, as if I can   look   hard enough
and trade this warm thrumming body

for a soft,   clean   shield;   a holy shelter of bones
cosmically shaped—hoped for, held, wanted—

from those mighty hands of the sky.

Wings

In the red dark womb
of my postpartum chrysalis

my body is magma.

Everything I know
about myself— the world
atomized — obliterated.

The sharp potency of my calcium bones
softened / suspended / dissolving like honey into tea.

I'm legs to wings
eyes closed, unwilling
and yet   *willing*.

I am unfolding
but still too sticky

yet to fly.

The chrysalis around me
a red placenta
grown from the grief /

the love

from my own anger / awe / and understanding

twisting atop each other
like wings

even as I am yet no butterfly.

Grieving the body I was

even as I

     lift

        off

            the

                ground.

Time Travel With Peaches - *September 2019*

I'm in the grocery store buying pectin, and I can't shake
my weariness, my blue shadowed exhaustion.

I call my mom while pushing the leaden cart.
"Can this still just be jet-lag after two days home?" I ask.

I am processing 50 pounds of peaches today,
and out of nowhere she quips, "peaches are great for growing

a baby." I laugh, ask if she has a sense of why I'm so exhausted.
The line is silent but it's a song

full of quiet knowing, hope and tension
and then she says: "Could you be pregnant?"

"No, I don't think so" I tell her, a surprising little smile
slipping out my lips and up onto my face.

A jolt of hope startling me along with
the sureness that I'm not, churning like butter in my belly.

"Better take a test just to be sure,
Peachy Girl," she tells me.

Hours later, I stand over the stick sure it would be negative,
but it's not.

Two fast fat pink lines and the room is spinning and I'm texting
my boyfriend, Ben, *come home.*

Knowing it's not enough.
But knowing it's got to be.

Venison

My skin is akin to a grape skin gone
blanched off and vanished
vital, like lungs, or a mom.

My muscles flex and the fascia is holding on
yet I have no barrier
between my beating, bleeding, breathing self

and the sun.

I'm in the grocery store staring at the pale nothingness
of chicken breasts
wrapped in plastic, packaged

in styrofoam. The big-throated screams
of a toddler two aisles over
runs like a razor right through me.

I feel like I don't have skin.

Nothing to protect my thin blue veins,
the blood running back to my heart.
Like a deer my mother and I

hit one night
coming home in our family's Volvo
station wagon.

An hour later, we strung her up
in the shop beneath a worklight
her tender limbs still warm,

her blood pooling thickly on the floor.
That oxygen red
that had been throbbing with blue life just hours before.

I can't forget the rasping sound of her skin
giving way under the knife
as we exposed the barren beauty

of her silken body. Her muscles
pale and pink,
strong and perfect.

Standing in the meat aisle
dredging up ideas for dinner;
this is exactly how I feel.

Honey

We move slow in the thick sticky
sweetness of these early days at home together.

A sleepless sunrise that still feels like night, yet
the warmth sneaks in our window

to illuminate the mess
of our love and all our laundry.

The smell of newborn— that honeyed perfume— clings to
everything — a scent like yearning and *having*
all I've ever wanted in one tiny room.

I'm crying every day. I am dulce de leche
caramelized in love's thick heat.
There's blood in the toilet. And milk
on the sheets.

Our bodies move so slow —suspended things with paper-thin wings
caught in thick amber.

Some soul part of us fossilized,
here, forever.

Summer

Summer Solstice

We'd marked it on the calendar a year and a half before
Summer Solstice *Saturday* 2020

But in my dreams it hadn't looked quite like this.
In the morning light, I stand barefoot

in our tiny bathroom and cut his hair. Brown locks landing
on the blue and white linoleum of our old house.

Our eyes catch in the mirror for a moment,
crystal blue on green

warm rivers, braiding together, our chosen
confluence
in the summer sun.

We didn't tell anyone, besides my best friend Teya,
who showed up in a mask that couldn't contain her grin and

helped load the car with flowers and her black camera.
Ben in his brown suit and good dress shoes.

She gently did up the zip on my postpartum body, his grandmother's white
summer dress, the only thing that fits.

Sometimes Love cannot wait.

So we run away to the mountains.

An unsigned marriage license tucked between the seats
and a three week old boy in a blue bowtie sleeping

in the back seat. It's a luminous day,
gold and purple. People out on the side of the road

to watch the sun go down.
The longest day of this longest year.

Every day facing into the unknown
again, looking straight into the sun.

In the gravel parking lot, Teya puts flowers in my hair,
safety pins my lace cape-veil that I made from a curtain

I found at Goodwill to my dress
and helps me out into the middle of the meadow

towards the deepest love I've known in this life.

There is no music.
No call to rise.

But there is birdsong. Aspen leaves quaking green
above us with their unmasked applause.

I feel the soft touch of his sapphire eyes on my face
unflinching, neither of us looks away.

The little girl within me who
 has imagined this moment so many times is surprised

she doesn't miss the spectacle
but instead is sated, her heart throbbing and satisfied.

We stand together in the last gold light
of this longest day of the year.

Committing to our love as big as the light does.
Committing to the everydayness of our shifting seasons

this life together. Our vows

aren't written down; they are our diamond tears.

Anointed with kisses,
punctuated with the squalls of our tiny son asking for milk.

Google can't be your mom.

I know. Because I've tried.

It's easy to google how many cups to a quart
and how many quarts to a gallon
not so easy to google,   *why did you leave?*

I've asked so many questions.
My search history
reads like a wound, a raised white scar:

Video search: how to tell the 6 different types
of infant crying?
What do you put in your soup-broth, Mom, that makes it taste

like coming home? Taste like the feel
of your hand —soft on my forehead?
What to do for bleeding that won't stop, two months postpartum?

Are you really okay, Mom? Because I'm not okay.
How to self-diagnose postpartum depression
Was it love or something else (fear?) that broke you, made you run?

~~New mom groups~~
Virtual new mom groups

I can't feel you anymore.
Colorado Covid cases today by county
Are you sick? Are you dying?

EMDR therapists near me
What's the ratio of raisins to carrots in the salad you always make?
Nature preserve with walking trails near me

When did you say I should worm Aberdeen again?

Lullabies to sing
How did you make sleep happen so easily for us?
Bedtime routines.

Facebook Marketplace. White noise machines. Black-out curtains.
Did I do something to deserve this?
Do you miss me?

Google maps: map the route back home
Do you believe I deserved this?
Did I do something to deserve this?

Facebook Marketplace. New picture frames.
Home Depot: Gold Paint.
Why did you leave?

Podcasts about grief.
Thrift stores near me.

Invisible Metropolis

Everything I do is so easily undone:

The dishes. The laundry.
The week's groceries
bought and brought home. The toilet
cleaned. The water bill paid.

A meal once cooked
is then consumed.
Much like the black words
I put down on white paper.

Who comes back to revisit a certain line, or
a certain crusted dish, scrubbed clean
beneath the light
of the equinox moon?

My life is built
upon this impermanent sand;

each day shaping castles, cradles, breakfast,
a home, out of it with my bare hands
that the ocean then dissolves, carries away
over and over and over again.

I wash our clothes;
hang them in the sun.
Fold them into neat piles
like some ancient devotion.

The coming to it. Committing to it.
Watching my hands making something
out of the nothing
over and over and over again.
I rake the falling leaves, their fading colors a wash of grief

around me. I mow the lawn. Walk the dog. Check on my mother.
Check on my mother-in-law. I water and mulch the new tree.
Collect the seeds for next spring.

I feed and play and nap
and nurse and walk

my child
over and over and over again.

Until the day he will no longer be a child.
And what then?

Will my life still feel invisible
then? Or will all my days of impermanence

have amounted to something?
This golden thing:

my boy.

This whole human I have grown.
But then his life is his own.

What of mine?

Isn't life both just as big
and yet bigger than that?

The quiet search for meaning
while we have something to do with our beautiful hands?

My love, he goes off to work, builds airplanes;
steel and carbon fiber birds

things that have wings that have never yet taken to the sky.
And I'm jealous

because he builds permanence.
History.

While I build and rebuild
over and over and over again

this unseen metropolis
we exist in everyday.

Lucky

Green four leaf clovers on his gray boxer briefs
as he rocks our wailing son around and around

our house in the dark; exhausted protests slowly giving
way to the quiet relief of sleep.

From my soft vantage point in bed
I can't help but feel like I'm the luckiest woman alive.

This human. This man in all his
overworked exasperation and

thinning hair;
his humor and witty puns about cheese

when we should both be sleeping. His blazing eyes,
his hands that set me on fire

that also bring me back to safety
with just a touch.

Even on nights when the anger from work follows him
home like a stray dog

begging to be fed at the dining room table

I feel so lucky, it's all I can see
in the half light of our old messy house

through the haze of sleep deprivation
this sweet, wild, difficult and fleeting life

we build together, one precious   (sleepless)
day at a time.

SOS

Simmering in a hot saltwater sea of solitude.
My tired baby, soggy beside me.

I'm beyond exhaustion, treading water;
I'm filled with rage.
Just go to sleep, I tell him.
Because I can't sleep, if you don't sleep.

And there is no one else in this house
to call for help.
My mother's
name on my recent-calls list
dropped all the way to the bottom;

from back before
I birthed this tiny light of a human
who I love,
so goddamn much.

My body is our boat and my grief
—it's all the colors of the sea—
out here, I'm empty; so thirsty
but even the water that buoys us
has been salted.

From the Front Seat in the Goodwill Parking Lot

What's the plural of apocalypse? Looking down Broadway
the city is shrouded in the hips and lips
of burning California smoke

I taste it in the back of my raw throat,
rub my eyes as if they could make me see,
push away the dawnings of this reality.

Just fifteen minutes, I tell them, one hand outstretched,
for quiet. No to-do lists
or shouldering into a crowd, head bowed, masked up

no baby biting / baby whining, at my deflated breasts
bite marks
purple around the edges

of where I used to draw myself
like a chalk line /
I'm more fine

more obsolete / aerosolized / sensational
out beyond the confines
of just who I'm supposed to be.

What is the plural of apocalypse?

Isn't there only ever supposed to be just one?
Like a mother
or a sky.

We're all burning. The truth of our humanity revealed in the ashes /
the twisted bones and beams left smoldering
like rotting teeth.

I wish I had the answers,
but I sit in my quiet black car
and I breathe

the acrid smoke because it is the air.
But it's not enough
to stop me

giving thanks
for the silent space
within this moment.

The beauty that is captured in one raw
staggering breath. Fleeting and alive
as we all sit collectively

atop this wildly tilting planet
poised above the precipice
before we begin the great big downward descent

into the wild and precious
            madness
of whatever comes next.

What is the plural of apocalypse?

The Mother & The Murdered

The headline reads: "Psycho charged with murder
in connection to three piles of human remains"

He is just twenty-six.
And I am left with all these unanswered questions,
heavy like bodies

lying quiet
against my own.

How can one
be charged in connection? Is it like a power cord
illuminating the electric possibility between us?

How much of a human soul
is left in a pile of remains?

How is it that we go from humans
            to missing persons
                        to remains?

How did they die? Were they scared?
Did they know they were loved? *Were they loved?*
Did he cry or vomit after?
If he didn't, how did he know he was still
alive?

Did they have to wait long? Were they *warm* enough?

It must be my mother's mind to worry that
as if an extra sweater
or an extra hat could have kept them
from bleeding out, dismembered in a burn pit.

This man—
printed beneath his picture in black italic ink

it reads "psycho" like it was his god-
given name.

His eyes in the paper are dead and defiant,
but I wonder what he looked like
when he was six or six months.
Was he a colicky baby?

At twenty six, how did he come to be?
Not the place, not the house with the peeling paint,
but *the people.*

Who was his mama?
Did she bleed with relief when she birthed him?
Did she weep with joy at his tiny fresh face?
Did he know he was loved? *Was he loved?*

Did he know these people were?

How had he forgotten?

Sitting in my yard, I feel an ache
twist in my chest like the swallowed up scream
I don't know how to let go of
as I watch my son playing with a spoon
in the afternoon dirt.
He's naked

his soft new skin crusted in mud.
The sun in his wild hair.

That toothless smile like honey itself
that he throws over a shoulder at me,
before going back to the serious work of dirt.

I know I will give beyond the limits of myself
everything
— all my breath, my body, my mind — I'll give
right through the thin bottom of my bank account,

offer up every crumb of time that I have on this earth,
till my heart is overdrawn

to *love* and to protect

those chubby little awkward hands.
That little dimpled cheek.

The headlines feel like crows—
hundreds of cracked claws holding on
tight to the telephone wires.
Their murderous voices
raised like low rasps on the still air.

I feel them catch and tear at me
as if to split me open,

but I am already shattered;
a hundred pieces of a heart.

I am both the mother
and the murdered.

Both the human
and the remains.

I am both the crow and the rasping caw.

I am at once
the woman whom he pulled the plug from

and too,
I am his vomit / I am their blood / on my hands

at what I have just done.

Autumn

Pantoum for June

My mother left me after my son was born, on the first day of June.
Like the blue-purple of a bruise, though the pain was from her absence
rather than her impact.
My sturdy glass heart shattered all over the floor.
My bewildered tears, like salty bullets disappearing,
slipping effortlessly out through the opened door.

Like the blue purple of a bruise, though the pain was from her absence
rather than her   impact.
Fuck. I whisper like a damning prayer.
My bewildered tears, like salty bullets disappearing,
slipping effortlessly out through the opened door.
But in the blackness I come face to face with my own brute,
golden strength, something no one else can take.

Fuck. I whisper like a damning prayer.
What did I do to make this happen? How could I have seen it coming?
A coal train barreling at me down the tracks.
But in the blackness I come face to face with my own brute,
golden strength, something no one else can take.
Invisible bullet wounds exit me, my grief— a rainstorm leaving.

What did I do to make this happen? How could I have seen it coming?
A coal train barreling at me down the tracks.
My sturdy glass heart shattered all over the floor.
Invisible bullet wounds exit me, my grief—a rainstorm leaving.
My mother left me after my son was born, on the first day of June.

Questions For My Mom

Dear Earth,
how do you sustain it?
The constant giving

of everything.
The giving of a mother
your insides turned

out, your flesh turned
to milk turned
to blood,

turned back to dirt,
so your children
might not go hungry.

How do you sustain
the loneliness after
they've grown up and gone on?

Do you ache with their forgetting,
or are *your* memories
enough?

Dear Earth,
can I ask,
are you bitter?

Do you hold regrets
close to your granite bones?
Or

is it wilder than that?
Wider than
the sacrifice?

Is each breath exhaled
out on the thick purple evening air
a kind of love song

back to you?

Each pair of eyes
that close in the velvet dark,
bodies, breath, heavy and succumbing

to the deep
pull of sleep like an exaltation
—like a prayer?

Do you feel each bare
foot dancing upon your shell
like a benediction?

A quiet, tender
kind
of homecoming?

Dear Earth,
I'm singing to you tonight.
We wayward children

grown up and gone
on in our asphalt streets
and spiked heels

laughing,
grateful tonight
even if we've forgotten.

Impatient in so many ways
to come home to you
lay our bodies

in your ground and let
you love us back
to nothing

back to   everything.

The Life Raft

What do you throw to yourself
thrashing / choking / blind from the salt /
out in open water?

A blue pen, dripping ink onto a soggy page?

A bottle of red nail polish you and your grandmother
used to love?

A bed, complete with a green, queen-sized microfiber
blanket that quickly turns from a refuge
into a sinkhole?

My lungs are the only life raft.

I breathe in and out. In and out.
Riding the oxygen I get,
letting it flood me.

Day after day after day of *trying.*

I'm so tired I could sleep here on the floor of the bathroom
soaked in beer and toothpaste

wearing yesterday's leggings / not caring
because tomorrow comes anyway.

I watch us from eyes
safe and dry on the shore and also—

from out here with no horizon line—drowning

And yet:

the joy in my little boy's face as he discovers a video of a red panda
                              sniffing a rock with its arms in the air

                    The way his little mouth says *kombucha*
                    like it's a dream or a spell for happiness

my cold insides are buoyed, warming with his joy

while I still churn with this heavy stone
inside my chest as though

I am a wanderer in some distant land,
arrived,

unwanted

without papers.

Hungry

In the grocery store parking lot around quitting time,
my son in his car-seat,
we troll along in electric silence looking for a parking spot.

A sun-leathered woman is holding the hand of
a little brown child.
They are crossing the parking lot

in our path.
I slow
and yet, she locks seething eyes on me,

her mouth
spewing words at me
clearly guttural hate.

I can't really hear her words.
I feel tight surprise in my chest;
I have no idea what she thinks I've done,

and yet I keep my eyes on her eyes
not as a challenge,
though I do not smile.

I'm listening.
Watching.
Trying to understand.

She keeps speaking and I catch the recognizable shape of
Fuck you as it leaves her lips
like a bullwhip,

and I feel the venom
scraping against the soft
skin of my breast;

the tightness of all that anger
that has curled itself up
like a cat to sit on her chest.

I glance at the little boy
and his little numb face
and then back at her

looking still
though now I'm not breathing.
Trying to understand.

And then it's over.

We've passed each other,
and I find myself putting on my blinker
to depart the parking lot.

My skin is so translucent and tender
after two years of holding
a tiny, thin-skinned baby close

and never looking anyone in the lips
that I feel my face shake
and crumple.

Who are all these that we have forgotten—
that have fallen
through the cracks?

Mothers and three-job-aunties—
all the hungry
and the hateful.

Because no one has cared to help them cross the street.

I feel a sense of kinship, *almost,*

with this woman.
If I were braver or less impinged

would I scream at people in parking lots
rather than just into my pillows
like the pretty polite white lady that I am?

It's fine. We'll just have leftovers for dinner.

H

At physical therapy
an entire hour of hands
on the intersection of my back.

Touching iron cartilage, steel muscles,
my rigid ribs.
My flesh corset.

The whole hour, she rubs and stretches and my body holds fast
unable – unwilling – to shape shift into someone
who can let it go

can fall apart and risk
turning to goo
again.

I thought I was already a butterfly.
Why is grief the chrysalis?
Why must I keep returning?

I want wings.

At the end she uses KP tape and marks a big blue H
on my back
across my shoulders and spine

as though signaling the helicopter to land *here*
as though telegraphing the single word my body aches
for but refuses to let me say out loud

Help

Crumple

There was a mother in my hometown,
driving alone, when a fully loaded coal train
barreled into her at a crossing.

There were whispers then that she'd raced
the engine—willfully—
that she'd meant to get smashed.

It   crumpled   everything;
her brain,   her spine,
her red car like a beer can.

I wonder what it did to her heart?

I couldn't understand how folks would say
that she'd meant to do it
but somehow, today, I do.

There is a certain kind of numbness, a haze.
It lives heavy in the limbs, the hours ticking by like
other people's careless fingers

undoing everything I work so hard to make.
Reducing my being like clarified butter to the justs;

just   a woman
        just   a mother
                        absolutely nothing else.

I am: lightless mornings/ thankless laundry/ groceries too heavy
 to carry/ the vacuum sucking up my life through the hose in my hands/ one more
carpool pick up/ one more lunch to bag/ one more thing to put on the calendar/
the trash to empty and drag out to the curb/

I am drowning in the constant invisibility
of being   needed
yet consistently, effortlessly, overlooked.

I'm not planning to speed my car in front of a heavy freight train,
but I'd be lying if I said
I never thought about it.

What relief
to be relieved of the burden
of   deciding,   making,   holding, everything?

She didn't die in that train crash, that mother.
Afterwards, she was cared for by her husband,
by a nurse, spoon-fed by
her daughter,
her rolling-chair always with a place at the table,

but I'm not sure it gave her what she was really after.
Wasn't she still just a prisoner?
Waiting for someone else to free her
in some small bird way?

I want my worth
to be based on more than my own invisibility—
my own willingness to serve.

Each day, I wake and feel the same keening ache
not just to be looked at— but to be seen;

to feel I am wanted,
alive and messy, imperfect
and important

and real. The need for it / aching
like a bullet
biting deep in my gut.

The Great American PayWall

Postpartum depression is a bitch
a dog in heat, she whines
loud around my sense of self-
worth disintegrating out into the wilds.

Throat tight and hands sweaty
I make my body move   ask   find   *please god*
I   need   help.

Just over that way, they gesture without eye contact

a flicked thumb over a shoulder,
but I see not a doorway
just the guiltless stones
of The Great American PayWall.

Wide and round, a thousand pounds
laid purposefully atop each other.
A slot at the bottom for me to insert my credit card.

Just four hundred fifty dollars for the first initial visit.
Sorry, we don't take insurance.

If you can't afford to pay it, you can apply for assistance;
but you'll need to fill out these 304 forms with ink
the color of your own despair.

Fax them to this number.
Shout till your voice breaks, trying to be heard
through the plexiglass partitions and a mask,
just to get an appointment,
to get an appointment.

Trained professionals wait on the other side of the wall.
Warmth in their touch on my arm

as I cry; reaching with their moisturized hands
into folders for recommendations
herbs and medication,
their care palpable, more real to me
than the sunlight slanting
on their impossibly clean floors.

I stare at the blankness of the Great American PayWall.
How it sits so desperately unimpeachable.

Before my baby, I sat in windowless welfare offices,
food stamp forms before me,
exhausted officials
with overworked kindness in their lamp-like faces,
trying to offer me resources they themselves need.

This is America.

Somedays, I think it looks easier to just scale
the fucking wall with a grapple in the dark
with my baby strapped to my back.

But I know they would gun me down,
watch us drown,
call us dogs, without a second thought.

So instead I sink down in the shadow of the stones
and feed my child from my sagging breast
and then

I pay the fee and log on.

I Go to the Thrift Store Looking for My Mom

As if I'll find her

lost between someone's floral queen sheet
set and a dish towel calendar
proclaiming it to be 1991 when I was still a soft round baby
snuggled up in the crook of her freckled arms.

I go to the thrift store looking for my mom.

It's where I learned from her how to brave.

Where I watched, her drab khaki pants drop to the floor
of the fitting room,
soft thighs that would one day look just like mine,
trying on power suit jackets and floral dresses after

we'd left my dad.
Her face in the mirror, hungry for herself
for the first time in my living memory,
deciding just who she dared to be.

I go to the thrift store looking for my mom.

That winter when I was twelve, on our way to California,
we stopped at so many thrift stores.
We'd sit together in what had been our family's
beige volvo station wagon,

counting out our cash into her small red fanny pack.
She'd look in the rearview
just so she could look herself in the eye
and say it aloud for me too: *we deserve this.*

We deserve this.
Then we'd go in.

Undoing the years of being told that our wanting was the problem.
Not the deprivation.

I go to the thrift store looking for my mom.

Thrifting has always been our church;
the sacred scent of cigarettes and sweat,
fluorescent lights flickering as holy as a votive
against stained glass windows.
It's where we learned to lay

our big, raw, hoping selves across the altar
of the check out counter.
Our dog-eared dollars exchanged for the possibility
of a *good life* contained in those white plastic bags.

I go to the thrift store looking for my mom.

Desperate to find that possibility again;
as if I could pick up the green rotary phone priced at $2.99
and call her and she'd answer
like it's five or fifteen years ago.

I'd tell her about the teal fairy princess dress I just found,
that I wouldn't have already outgrown.
But the silence now, between us, it's too big, too broken,
like a wedding dress ripped that I alone cannot re-sew.

I go to the thrift store looking for my mom.

She used to tell me she'd go to thrift stores when she was lonely
for me when I was living in New York.

As if we could connect through the racks and hangers,
the wires of love and second hand clothes.

I now know the insides of all the thrift stores

within a 40 mile radius of my home.
I go to the thrift store looking for my mom.

But I do not find her.
Instead I stand with strangers, other people's mothers
who ask me kind nothings about my little blue-eyed son.
I answer them and try to smile, out of practice,

their easy kindness, awkward, against my daughter's yearning
for my mother,
her sweet holy water hands.

While I stand in the aisle with strangers and my thirsty bones burn.

I go to the thrift store looking for my mom.

She hasn't died, but that sacred life between us
is now just a radio turned to static
where there used to be only   our favorite   songs.

Maybe I've driven too far outside the reach of
that radio station
living in the suburbs with my husband,
or, maybe she did;

when she drove away from me without warning,
leaving me like donations
standing in my driveway
with my four-day-old baby in my arms.

Making Sure

Walking the cement streets with my dad where I've made my home, hundreds of miles from the familiar heads of the mountains I was born from. One hand pushes the stroller and my father speaks— his leather steps whispering on sidewalk—as he spills his stories from the precipice of his eager lips. Opinions sharp with both / hope and disgust / for this our modern, apocalyptic world. Phrases like: "global psychosis" "electric-car mania" tumbling from his excited tongue—he dreams of owning a Tesla, being fully self-sufficient, charging from his own solar panels—he speaks as though he can taste it, as though it fills some hungry void inside him / with food. And I don't know which it is—him seeing a world waking up around him, *finally,* or if he feels like the only one awake in a desperately sleeping world.

His words shake, as if it's shaking the facia of his bird body. And when asked if he still has PTSD from flying helicopters in Vietnam, he pauses and looks into the pale boneless sky and says "You just have to reframe everything – in order to let yourself live / with it." And I think about all the things he must have reframed. All the things he's urged me— so ardently—to reframe in my thirty years alive. All the things my body remembers [so vividly it makes bile rise in my belly]. Things he must have reframed over and over again until he reframed it right out of existence. Out of breath. Out of white cloud memory.

Horrific pain does that to a person. It's how we survive. *Isn't it?*

I watch him seeking over and over again the electric warmth of— belonging—past the place of shame—that place that lights up in the center of your chest when someone knows and wraps their arms around you *anyway*. The eager face of a little boy—overlooked and underfed— peeking out from beneath his grizzled cheek as if to check if the world is still against him; or if the sun has finally come out.

I watch him play with my son. The way my child's eyes light up and the giggles erupt out of him—*pure unadulterated joy*—the love on both their faces dancing like candle light and I wonder how much is being healed—how much is being healed here— before it's ever even been broken? So long as I keep standing here watching. Listening.

Making sure.

Salt Water

Gasping out in open water
with the waves coming in

I feel like I can't possibly drink enough air
before my lungs fill with salty water again

over and over again
I resuscitate her / me / us

and over and over again
the water comes.

I'm drowning. I'm drowning. I'm drowning.

And there is no one here to hear me

gurgle and struggle and sink
because that's the thing with drowning, isn't it?

The real thing isn't messy
and loud and obvious

it's quiet and insidious and happening.

I listen to ocean waves at night
to help the baby sleep

and yet
all I hear

are my bones
crashing

tumbling
breaking

open
on an empty beach somewhere

pounded in the churning
burbling

depths of a hungry wild salty surf.

The Cost

I don't even let my mother-in-law inside my house
to see her grandbaby—she walks the cancer wards
at the hospital—and the risk is too great—both ways.

Yet the repair-man charges inside my house today
to look at my busted stove

tells me with an unbothered shrug of his blue-clad shoulder
that he and his family didn't have *no socially distanced thanksgiving*
and he rolls his eyes
not like that Damn Governor asked us to do

I step back, in my mask, my baby strapped to my back,
and I wonder, distantly, seethingly,
why is it that middle-aged white men
feel it is always appropriate to assert their politics
into polite conversations?

I don't even let myself call
my best friend, ask her inside
even on days when I feel I have nothing left to give
to my child;
I am a rock: giving blood,
offering breast, but it's just bone.

The repair man complains about the lag time in getting parts, how
the stove company is still only letting people work *at half capacity*
—and I think about my friend, a nurse who gave up her space
in safe, sparsely-populated Colorado to work in the trenches
of New York City, how her face lost all it's blood as she recalled
the stacks of body bags, the refrigerator trucks lined up in the street,
their black backdoors open, the mouths of morgues.

I stand at the stove speechless, my throat so tight
as this repair-man looks at me with his watery eyes

and tobacco stained fingers and sells me
a replacement part for three-hundred-dollars
that *I could have bought myself* online for twenty.

Everything about this,
the cost of this visit,
too   high.

But I smile tightly from behind my mask
remembering how my politeness
is owed
to men
who endanger me;

I've been taught to nod along and smile
and to take the three-hundred-dollar part

if it will *fix* it.

Wild Horse *or* Rodeo Queen

How many wild horses do you have? A pair of two? Ten?
A hundred?

Tonight I stand with four hundred
wild horses, stamping their feet and snorting.
There is a black thunderstorm coming
and not adequate fencing
and I stand—my arms spread, my eyes wide—daring
them to try it— my body a cracked blue rubber band
holding the whole fucking world together.

Except my wild horses are a list of mortgage
payments, covid tests and water bills;
a child in need of a nap,
a husband in need of friends, or a hobby, a sense of self or sleep—
I can't breathe.

It's so familiar to feel the lead vest of the world wet
upon my shoulders.

I got this—I say under my breath— staking myself
in the open gap of the broken gate—the way I watched my mother
a rodeo queen hold back the hordes— as I send my husband
up to bed in the silence and velvet
darkness of our guest room;
while I clean the stained white countertops of our old kitchen,
feed the scraps of today to the dog,
sooth and shoosh my son who has awakened in the dark,
offer him the milk of my breast
the honey of my quiet murmurs until he sleeps
and I am

alone   again
with the horses.

Wasn't I a wild horse once upon a time?

Barefoot rambling, muscles rippling, effortless
through desert orchards,
eating apples?

Why am I trying to hold wild horses back,
who belong out there
on the wild land they were made from

free?

Wind Chimes & White Cake

My feet whisper along the silver sidewalk;
my son, sleepy but not sleeping tucked against
my skin.

We travel in the velvet gaps
of darkness, through spills of street lamp light
like milk.

Yet, somehow
tonight I can't shake this feeling that we are
        traveling

              slipping

        between a fold in the veil
of time / of this reality / that we walk through a very different neighborhood
tonight.

The streets aren't wide
and empty but tight, littered with empty-handed
children.

The wind picking over gutters strewn
with glass, the sharp glitter
of needles and dark rubbish;

I can smell deep rot and human waste.

Dogs bark like a wild wide roar against
the ping of a chain link fence
and thud from behind triple bolted wooden doors.

As we cross the street,
I feel the hair raise upon my arms and neck
and *my other eyes*

catch a glimpse of the steel
flesh of a gun
pulled beneath the street light.

I freeze in the middle of the street.

I can feel the heat of it—I've walked between them—
aimer and target and I am caught
tasting the metallic tang of

fear deep in my throat.
My infant son strapped to my chest,
my arms around him

a shield
but what good is my body's boundary,
my protection,
when I hear

the trigger? Pop. The crack
splitting the air
like the Fourth of July.

The dogs go quiet
as the bullets,
just as they were
meticulously designed to do
break

into us.
Shredding baby Bjorn carrier.
Shattering bone.
Piercing our
tender bodies like

white cake.

My body
doesn't know
what to believe,

which eyes to look from. I can't
breathe but
I'm walking now,

blindly,
in the dark.
My arms still wrapped

around my child,
the vital air
in my lungs

trapped and
desperate for escape.
My freckled body rigid with fear.

Yet, the most menacing thing we've come across tonight
is someone's wind chimes
on their empty porch

tinkling
on and on

though there is absolutely no wind.

We are alone on the street.
But I can't close my eyes on it.
I know

those bullets
have buried themselves,
and there is blood everywhere
staining the sidewalk red-brown.

A Mother's keening wail tearing open the sky;
staining all of our hands.

I carry the grief
  [is it her grief?]
heavier than my child
who finally sleeps.

I tell myself,   *will myself,*
to come back,   come home
                                    completely.

I open our unlocked front door.
Flick off the porch light,
climb into the warm bed beside my safely sleeping husband.

Beyond our wordless window,
the night is silent and still
no wind.

I close my eyes,
yet I can't get my *other eyes*
to stop seeing.

Stop knowing.

Stop weeping.

Mother to Mother in the Grocery Store after you lost your baby at 20 weeks

I listen to the topography in your voice,
the story you slowly tell me, under fluorescent lights.
It's so much more than dates and doctors and who
was there—it's the way your body breathes you in

and out and I climb
the steel sharp mountains of emotion with you.
Jagged like breath / like sobs
that break / at the beaches of unshed tears

my hands outstretch / touching your arm
despite everything / you're still warm.

My body is an autonomic barometer,
my nervous system, a mirror for the storm / I watch
crossing you / gooseflesh erupting

up each of our spines
with the rain,
the hail that comes as you talk;

the way, as you spill the words,
your hands run themselves
across your old hopes / across
the dried-up river bottoms—where ducks
and deer and birds used to gather
elegant necks extended / reflected on the water.

Now there's nothing here— the land bone
dry— just this fine brown grief-silt—
heavy on your palms.

Between your syllables
I hear the thick emerald pines of your longing

that light up my belly—and yours—with the agony

and with the remembered yellow
of joy — that heart-ripping hope— of holding
her little body against yours;

breathing in   life together.

That longing, I hold you as
you hold it,

as it holds you
like the fingers of two hands
twisting atop each other
            reaching   reaching.

They play Bohemian Rhapsody over the market's sound system.
Somewhere, out there, it's time for dinner.

Winter

The Battlefield Blackout

█████████children
█████wounded██████
█████
███████████

want their Mothers

████████████Mothers;
███████████████
██████████████████████
█████████████
█████ unable to breathe.

████████████████████████
█████global pandemic.
We stayed inside ████████
████████████████
██████████████████

█████████████
███ my body
█████ a stronghold, ████████
██████████████████
█████

██████████

I remember ████████████
█████ their eyes
███ soft, ████████████████
██████████████ the edges
of myself;
██████████████████
███ blurry ████████
█████ giving ███████ anything
██████████████

74

my body

the striking point

slippery

stretching　　so thin　　the light

tore open

new configuration

of woman.

in　darkness

my Mother

a light

love ▮ ablaze

massive

the heat

inside of her

cracking,   shattering

heart,

untouched

Roaring.

s   h e
w   ent

her silent engine

too close

burn

heart / breath

throbbing
caught

feral motherhood

please, ▮▮▮ *don't let us drown.*

▮▮▮▮▮▮▮

▮▮▮▮

▮▮▮▮▮▮▮

▮▮▮▮▮

▮▮▮▮

▮▮▮▮▮▮

▮▮▮▮ stop ▮▮▮▮

▮ the girlish blood ▮▮▮▮▮▮

▮▮▮

▮▮▮

▮▮▮

▮▮

▮▮▮▮▮

▮▮▮

▮▮▮▮

▮▮▮▮

▮▮▮▮ teach myself

▮ to walk again.

How to hold ▮▮▮ my ▮▮ raw, real self

▮ her ▮▮▮▮ b▮e▮

▮▮▮ loved.

▮▮▮▮▮▮

▮▮▮▮▮

▮▮▮▮▮

I. ▮▮▮

▮▮

████████ do ████

████████████ this.

████████████████

████ breath in my ███ chest

████ give it ██ my ███ child, ██████ breathe.

████████████████

Stone Soup

When I was a child, my mother used to tell the story of stone soup:
how you add water and a rock to a pot and somehow you'll
get thick fragrant broth because of all the things your neighbors bring.

I'm hungry. I'm so hungry. But my neighbors are away. And
I've been making stone soup all year.

Salt from my tears / from my sweat /giving every goddamned thing
I have / to keep our family floating out here on the open ocean.

No sleep / no knocks at the door / no offers of *let me hold the
baby, you go take a nap /* or, *oh hey, I made you dinner.*

Instead it's masks / and mass shootings, stress and sweat and
one fucking foot in front of the other.
Learning how to walk in my unbalanced body again.

My family laughs when they text. *So grateful for all the pictures,*
they write, as if there is no brokenhearted subtext.

I wonder how much stone soup my mother made?
How many nights we ate gravel and hot salty water
and how many nights she wished we were all eating

something more?

Peanuts

My Delaware grandmother, Nanu, used to send us
Christmas in a cardboard box.
On the morning of the twenty-fifth

we'd huddle around the fire
in our thick thirdhand coats
and crack it open with a sharp knife.

One wrapped present for each of us,
usually socks, tucked between back issues
of *Reader's Digest* and Irish Spring soap,

tubes of Crest toothpaste
and opened bags of pretzels and potato chips
sitting in their deflated silvery shrouds

long gone stale in the heavy, wet, east coast air.
As though we were an outpost
of US soldiers, refugees,

Out West
beyond understanding and in need
of anything.

I never watched my father's face
when we opened this cardboard cornucopia
from his mom.

But there was something in his jaw
that tightened
but never spoke.

When she died,
my dad didn't cry
just urged my oldest brother and I, both now adults,

to finish our goodbyes
and get back to our pew
so they could crank the coffin closed.

My dad spent that weekend alone
in her old red brick house,
the one he had grown out of boyhood in.

Finally, eating crumbling things in every room.

//

Tonight, my dad visits me at our house on Delaware street,

sitting easy at our kitchen table.
The delight in my son's face calling out "Pappy;"

the first time my dad's heard it in person
though he only lives a handful of hours away.

My dad arrived with *gifts*.
Half his dusty disused pantry in a cardboard box:

Jars of his beloved mayonnaise / packets of expired shelf stable
cheese / winter greens my mother grew in the cold frame—which I
devour straight from the bag /boxes of expired meals I recognize
as gifts I once brought him before their sell-by-date.

He fills my fridge
with leftovers once frozen in someone else's freezer
now perspiring in puddles in mine.

Despite bringing so much sustenance
with him, he sits at my kitchen table and waits
for   me   to make him every single meal.

He leaves without warning
on a Saturday morning,
and he leaves all of the food behind.

"*You need it,*"
he says as he puts on his shoes,
and I feel sick with his going

like we could have been more together
and also relieved in the marrow
of my bones.

And I think about all the ways our family is uncomfortable with *I see
you,* with saying the words *I love
you,* with looking the truth square in the eye.

But how we're not afraid to leave opened bags of peanuts
and pretzels on the counter,
and leftovers in the fridge

like some sweating piece of a heart.

Ready?

She asks as I stack the towels in the closet.

Ready?
She asks as I turn out the light and climb beneath the weight
of winter blankets.

Ready? She asks.
Her spirit alive with the urgency of longing to become.

Ready?
But I am not ready.

Yet, she comes anyway.
Two pink lines on a pee stick. Ben and I are looking at each other
with wide open eyes.

Ready? We mouth to the other.

But it turns out none of us are ready.

Red Spring Run Off

I get up in the dark
morning and there's a smear of red
blood on the white
toilet paper;

a flag
signaling trouble.

There is nothing to do—
they tell me when I call,
so I start a load of laundry
piling the socks and sheets
into the big white machine.

The agitation sending
tiny tremors throughout this body
of my house.

drip.
drip.
drip.

I make breakfast.

I crack the eggs into the black heart of the frying pan.
I watch the heat take and transform the golden yokes
slowly making
the soft edges hard;
baptizing its blonde potential
into fuel.

drip.
drip.
by precious red drip.

I curl my freckled body around the soft
sharp reality of my toddler.
Breathing in his fading baby scent.

Letting the bones we made together jostle this
house of my body
in the middle of all this losing.

I feel the pull inwards;
my spine begins to curl
a fern; my bones growing soft
my spirit folding in on herself
beneath the tender enclosing weight

of the chrysalis.

I'm not ready *and yet*
I go under anyway.

My body pulled like a ribbon
whipped on a wind that carries the ancient song
of this matriarchal music;
so many hundreds of thousands of women's voices
lifted in grief together.

It's time for the red spring run off now,
though it's only February.

My shuffling topside body
only enough
to fill the dishwasher with empty things.

I am awake only
in the depths of the underworld
whispering into the hair of the women-goddesses
I trust:

I lost the baby.

And their wails echo in the canyons
of their cave hearts and
their wails are my wails.

I stand at the bottom of the bottomless cave
letting myself
feel

grateful

for all her molecules
still swimming
inside me;

in my blood
and in my brain.
All the ones I get to keep.

The ones that stay with me
long after her tiny
wing-tipped body is gone.

Red River Jade

I picture her,
freckles and a wild tangle of red hair.
Her willful delight at being bare in the sun
no matter how much it burns her—

her laughter like spring—like sun on snow melt,
water fresh and bracingly cold.
The only thing that could quench my thirst
though I didn't realize my own dehydration until I felt her.

I love her.

Translucent and warm and unable to hold
though she is now;

I love her.

She came but couldn't stay.
A note left scrawled on my soul self's door

hey, get ready
hey, I'm coming

Make a little more room for me, please;
make a little more room for *you.*

As if, between the two of us
we can shift the weight   for / from   our ancestors;
the women before us who birthed alone
in hospitals and huts
who shrank themselves down until they were nothing
but an empty mantle for the words: motherhood.

Make a little more room for yourself, Mama

because *you* need it, and I, I'm going to need every
square inch of it too. *You walk Mama, and I will run. Dance. Twirl. Burn.*

Together, we will create change.

I feel it. I feel the rooms I have to build within myself
for her. For all of us.
I want to do this.

She told me her name in the middle of the night
after she'd touched my womb with her body
and then rode the red river out.

I surfaced from a dream
the grief like a veil around me
and she told me: *my name, this time, Mama,
is Jade Alexandria.*

My daughter
free.

Fluorescent Green Grief

Heavy, I stand staring at the frozen food section of the grocery store
glassy eyed, trying to decide
what to get for dinner.

Each inhalation feels like a soggy, steep mountain to climb
my weary bones lifting just enough to get me through this
maybe enough, in time
to get me home.

Grief. I huddle beneath her
in the fluorescent green light
her arms like concrete wings around me,

sturdy. I'm grateful for the KN95 mask
that shields me and the tears,
my mouth wide and gaping in the grief I can't contain.

I am overfilled, without skin.

You're doing a good job, I tell her / me /us
my open hand a metronome on my chest.

You're doing good, I whisper in the check-out line
desperate to get back home and back into the arms of my
bruise-black bed.

Due Date

On Jade's due-date on the beach in California,
I write her name in the wet sand.

As the sun sets and the waves crash,
the sky turns a riot of purple and blood orange.

I complete the final A in Alexandria and
take a breath, standing back to look at it
and that's when the waves come up strong and gentle
and disappear all that I have written.

So brief.
Her name stayed with us
yet so right;
that the ocean would come to wipe it clean
and take her home;

the way the red waters of my womb did
just the same.

Learning How to Sisterhood

In our leggings and bare chests between the gorse bushes
we howl
our voices free-flying against the silence of an ancient glacier
the umber mountain scarred and smoothed from hundreds of thousands
of years of ice
we stand naked with our heat (and our different mothers
and absent or angry fathers)

the flames that have lived for centuries in these veins
the wild raw redness inside like a dragon or a ribbon
lifted and whipped on the ancient wind.

What is sisterhood someone asks.
Let's define it.
Pin her dead body down like a jeweled butterfly in a box

but I don't need a manifesto or a bullet point list
I want what we already have.

This. The raucous laughter that erupts after the howling
arms that yearn to reach out and hold
no matter the distance between bodies
between hearts, aching or uncertain or jubilant.

I want this, the fridge that won't close,
because we've all brought too much food to feed each other
just for the weekend.

I want these belly laughs that feel like they might break me
break something old and senile that's lived too long rent free within me
I even want the squirm in my belly, that ancient ache,
when I look into the zoom screen and I'm more seen
more intimate than looking in a mirror

I want the nights of backless dresses and days of sweatpants and unwashed hair

92

and no we don't care, do you want something to eat?
I want the fashion trends that come and then go

I want time.

Time as I watch the world deepen the laugh lines around your eyes
as I watch you want so much,
some you get and some you don't
but I see inside your eyes there's still the essential wildfire
of who you are.

I want this
undefinable because sisterhood
she changes. Grows.
Get's divorced. Cuts off all her hair. Moves to a new city. Expands.
Dreams. Has a baby. Starts over. Falls in love.
Yet remains gloriously alive
in this belonging.

She's right here, a heartbeat beneath the skin
of my freckled fingers as I reach for you

and you
and you
and you reach for me too.

This is sisterhood

Acorn

I dug a hole beneath our maple tree with a sharp trowel,
and we placed the fleshy bits I'd passed inside it
along with the acorn that the oak tree in Illinois had dropped
onto my belly like a blessing
even as I was bleeding.

We did this together
as a family
beneath a sky the color of tangelos and the fleshy inside
of a pink grapefruit.

Ellis asked why we were doing this
and I told him
*because we thought we were gonna have a baby but it turned out
this baby couldn't stay.*

I'm sad, he says,
watching the tears slide down my face.
Me too buddy,
I tell him.
Me too.

Empty *or* Thanksgiving

I lost another baby—this time I think a boy—
I've nearly stopped bleeding now

my very bones are tired from holding all
of this longing in

my arms ache to hold my child
his head nestled *here* against my heart

thump bump, thump bump
goes my fragile failing heart

there is no baby now
no due date to count towards

or friends to giddily tell with tears of joy
just my blood

coating the U bend
and a graveyard in my heart

I'm already prepping in my head the text I'll need to send
to prepare my family for thanksgiving

please don't ask again
if we're planning or pregnant

I'm trying — my metaphysical arms spread wide
to protect my paper-thin heart

so my words don't have to, so I won't have to speak
it over the hum of turkey and

green bean casserole
we've lost another baby.

The Lighthouse *or* Apology, Oregon

This morning my mom texts me from Apology
Oregon—*need anything from the thrift store?*—

her words an electric jump to my heart
too hot to hold, so I put my phone down.

All the lights suddenly flicking on; our lighthouse blinking
it's yellow beacon again against the blue-dark

to all the ships lost at sea.
And I'm angry—how effortlessly— she walks back in,

flipping some big breaker inside herself
that connects both our hearts
back to the ancestral grid.

When I was in high school, out late without a way to call,
I'd close my eyes, strike metaphoric match to candle
hold it up in the open window of our lighthouse,
don't worry Mama, I'm safe, I'll just be half an hour late.
Arriving home, she was never worried
because she always caught my light.

My body quakes at how *easy* it is
to be connected,
a spark leaping between cut wires,
so *ready* to make the connection.

But my body is a dusty box of relays, capacitors
paralyzed,   grateful,   hateful,   *hopeful*
spring arriving too early in my heart, buds bursting
still with the threat of snow.

My mom texts me from Apology
Oregon—but with no apology— just
some questions about jackets.

And I wonder is she back for real this time?
I lost another baby last week.
Blood coiling in the toilet
and she didn't feel it, the windows dank and empty on the cliffs.

Yet, today she texts me about the sunrise
while I'm watching the colors streak my sky

and now it's afternoon and I'm undressing for the shower—
the sharp spark of remembrance hits me, *I never responded*
before my fingers can open the app
her name is appearing like an apparition—this time texting about
something else—but I felt the beam blind me before her SMS found
me.

And I feel so naked—I want to laugh
and tell her I feel her again
but even that feels too vulnerable
like I've been at the window waiting this whole time, like a dog.

I yearn to sit in the yellow lamp light of her love.

I am keening to be held against the warm familiarity of her heart,

yet I know I am a different person now,
            my self a different size
all the places I had to grow,
in order to survive.

What happens if I open my book of matches
if I try,
by the time I make it across this four year forged canyon in my heart,
will our lighthouse still be burning brightly in the dark?

Only later do I realize she hasn't texted me from Apology
Oregon —because that town doesn't exist— instead
she texted me from inside Anthropology
and her phone autocorrected it.

Yellow

Sitting in the diner on Main Street,
over cold eggs and the dregs
of tea I keep re-hearing the sound

my best friend makes

when my mother shows her
the picture on her yellow phone
of her cancer.

"Woah-ah" —too big— all of what she's feeling
it won't fit in a single word
a single syllable,

and I think about how much trust
it takes to show someone your cancer,

and how much bravery
it takes to look at it.

Such fragile milk-white life
laid out on the formica table top along with the ketchup;

like looking in through the white bars
of ribs

directly at the heart.

Clean

I stalk around my house with the all-purpose spray and a rag
hunting for things to clean,

to scrub back into some kind of wholeness,
some type of submission or peace

as if I can make us all
better—

kinder, cleaner, more able to love,
be loved, heal, with just

enough of my women's willpower,
my spray bottle of soap,

my ardent elbow grease,
my desperate delusional hope.

Whiteout

I like it when it snows, when it's a complete whiteout.
When the world is made small like a snow globe
and strangers smile at each other,
pushing slipping cars out of snowdrifts just to get home.

I like it when it snows, when it's a complete whiteout,
when you can't leave, but it's okay, because you don't want to.

I like it when it snows, when it's a complete whiteout.
The windows of the black truck we pass each morning
on our way to preschool, with the bumper sticker
of the AR-15 and the words *come and take it*
expunged away with softness; like they don't exist.

I like it when it snows, when it's a complete whiteout.
Even in a complete black-out the snow acts like lanterns
lighting the night with the softness of their frozen souls;
like maybe after we die we all get a turn as a snowflake.
Remembering how to fly   how to fall
remembering what it's like to be one small,
                                soft,
                                        part of
                                                winter.

        Together, covering the land.

Drop off

He sits in the sun on the circle carpet / idyllic and animated telling
his preschool teacher
all about the rocket he is building out of connector blocks.

I have already said goodbye. Given fifteen squeezes that feel sweet,
and too rushed,
loving and not enough. Like these years we get together.

But I stand in the doorway, drinking up the sight of him /
the miracle of my son. One last sip
before the day / begins to eat / our hours / our minutes / this
childhood.

Teaching each of us to bite down through the softness / of ourselves
until we hit / bone.

My day ahead is hungry / waiting / already wailing
for me in my pocket /
yet I'm crying— never a morning without knowing
how these squeezes could be our last.

I walk out into the bright white oblivion of the parking lot
and ask myself, is it enough? Have I done enough?

Loved hard / fought big
enough for a world / in which, whoever my son becomes / is safe?

I watch the other mothers leave the parking lot
in their exhales and empty cars and wonder if they feel it too?

If they're just as eaten up by it?
If they're just as starving / as malnourished

by this low-carb, no-fat, all-american mother's
diet we each swallow
day in, day out,
like a bullet.

It's January and the Birds are Literally Saving My Life

I look up from the doldrums of the white day
January spread thin
over my calcium bones.

The birds are flocked against the sky;
seagulls wheeling in January,
snowstorm flurrying around them
and they don't care.

So alive, together
their beating wings
soaring.

As if there is no massacre.
As if genocide doesn't exist.
As if I don't risk our lives every time I take my child to school
and leave him there.

It's January and the birds are literally saving my life.

My therapist tells me that listening
to birdsong is the best thing we can do
for our ancient mammalian vegas nerve;

we have woken up with the birds
for millions of years.
Our first alarm,
the system that went silent if
the unthinkable was near.

It's January and the birds are literally saving my life

Reminding me to look up;
that is where the rain and grace,
 snow and hope and sun will all come from.

I think about the pigeons years ago
winged doves, white, winging against the sky.
A hundred of them, the motion of their beating bodies together.
A song we can see.

How my mom and I stood shoulder to shoulder
And watched them wing
every morning for a week;

goosebumps rippling between us;
a squeeze or two of our reverent hands.

Just to watch this world being alive

while we're alive
together,
in it too.

Spring Again

Peonies

I ink my body with flowers;
wear them to the funeral of my former self,

sit at the tombstone of that soft, silent girl
who always nodded yes and smiled when she said no;

who quaked at the thought of burning her blank canvas body
with blooms   *because what if*

someone—a casting director or a worthy man—
could only love her if she came like cotton

stretched clean across oaken bones
unmarked, but ready

to be perfectly projected upon.

It's just an empty white envelope of body,
buried, down thick in the brown soil now.

I can't leave her *these* flowers.
I have to take them with me;

have to let this body keep growing
get louder /
         go wild /
                  go *positively*
                              to seed.

Bird

Bawling broadway roars her rush-hour aria
black pitted asphalt crunches in the thick evening heat

A hawk, talons tight
eyes like black beads
high in a dark cottonwood tree

The micro movements of her muscles flex as she shifts
like a silver mirror of my own ankles
as I balance the bike

red plastic dog lead taught in one hand
leaning my freckled summer body
around the blue bulk of the baby-seat
angling myself against
my son

Our sun warmed faces, close
full of wonder
as we look up

and he taps his thumb and forefinger
together excitedly
making the sign for
                                        bird

Can I come for a visit?

My mother texts me out of the blue
on what would have been Jade's 2nd birthday.
I can feel the moment draw it's breath
around me, my heart tight,

ravenous

for a benediction.

I know about heavenly magic,
even if she hasn't asked to come
back in over four years.

I text her back:

Yes, okay.

Goodwill

After school drop-off I ask her what she wants to do
she cocks her head at me, smiles in that achingly
familiar way
and says: *Goodwill?*

I drive her to my favorite one. It has a view of the mountains
from the parking lot.

When we walk in I feel weightless, like we've time traveled,
my heart so hungry, over so many solo trips,
just for this.

We piece through circle racks,
and I can feel her thrumming body warm beside me
without even looking;

feel my own body solid in my shell;
that old easy awareness of each other
a private language warm— a mother tongue— spoken
easily again
after these long four years.

It's almost Halloween, and we are captivated by the costumes
circling round the racks
running thumbs and fingers over velvet and silk,
the occasional scab of leather, a buckle, synthetic straps.

I find the most hideously adorable unicorn outfit
for a toddler, garish pink horn sits atop grey hood
but somehow it's still so cute.
I take it round to show my mom, grinning
as she's pulling the same unicorn onesie
from the masses of costumes, her's in an adult size large to show me.

Now we're really laughing. Giggles erupting
up out of each of us
as do the goosebumps.
Our eyes catch, hold, aquamarine blue on green.

My heart—glad, pounding—
heaving   up   the breaker
to turn all the lights on
inside   me too.

Isn't it Schrödinger's cat who is both dead and alive? Isn't it
Glennon Doyle who says we can hold two truths at the same time?

This light in our lighthouse is burning bright again.
Yellow-gold winging away across the purple water.

It does not heal all the time I've spent alone in the dark.

But / it feels so good / to just sit in the glow / again
of each other.

Peachy

Each morning I place these minutes behind museum glass.

My mom sitting with her tea steaming at my kitchen table,
asking my son curious questions,
his answers coming thick and fast.

I want to be able to come back and revisit these hours,
sit slow
and savor them in their easy light.

My mom letting out a whoop of joy
as she tries my electric bike.

I touch these moments carefully.

Standing in the parking lot of Trader Joe's
the cancer swelling on her cheek;
"I know it'll make me cry" she says
"but I have to say this, I have to speak"

I want to rerun this moment like a reel,
feel the film slippery between my fingers,
my galloping cardiac:

Peachy Girl, I'm so sorry.

I'm sorry. I'm sorry I left you,

and that I didn't come back.

I touch the moment tender in my mind.
Try not to disturb the dust.

Let there be enough room for the love

and the loss

and us.

Waist Deep

I am alive and waist deep
standing in the salty waters of my matriarchal lineage.

I heave up from below my DNA, memories and slippery forms
asking to be lifted
asking to finally float free in the buoyancy of this little wooden boat
that I steady with one hand.

The things we've passed to each other
the women in my family
unknowingly like a relay

It's not just my grief.
It's our grief

that's seeped into each of us as we steeped
in the warm amniotic fluid of each other

the oocyte of me weightless inside my mother's forming body
at twenty weeks while she floated, still forming, inside my
grandmother Mary—the one I never got to meet.

In my therapist's office, I lean forward
my body shaking but hot with *yes*
that I accept / am ready for / call in
the weight of this matriarchal grief.

It's not just me who became a mother alone.

My own mother, Lucy, standing with my begrudging father
in the Baton Rouge justice of the peace
eight months pregnant with my brother in a white nightgown.
While the radio played *"Under my Thumb"* by the Rolling Stones
and they had to find the janitor to sign the witness line.

A week after my brother was born,
my dad got a call that his youngest brother and favorite person alive
had been killed in a car crash. His brother was seventeen.

Six weeks later, sitting in my grieving grandmother's house,
my postpartum mother's heart alarm went off.
She ran upstairs to the red room to find my brother,
blue and unmoving, curled into a tight ball.

She says both their lives flashed before her eyes and
time stopped, her body took over and she
blew on his face, willing him to come back to his body
if he could.

*I let my body shake with the sobs as I imagine laying
that terror down,* her terror down
inside this boat.

My mother's mother Mary was twenty-three
when she gave birth to a baby girl
while my grandfather was away at sea.
Three thousand miles away from home
the doctors left the room, spoke in hushed, hurried tones
but wouldn't tell her why,
"Just don't feed the baby."

But little Jamey Jennifer was crying, hungry
so my grandmother Mary picked her up
and put her to her breast
 and then Jamey   started   drowning.

The tubes that should have connected mouth to belly instead
sunk all that glorious milk directly
into her lungs.

She lived three days.

My body shakes. Unthinkable.
Mary, going home alone without a baby
to a cold house on the water with an empty bassinet waiting like a joke.

Is there a grave I could visit with her?
Put my flowers down
like I place the purple and fuchsia petals
of this grief? I say their names.
 Lucy. Mary. Jamey. Put it all into the boat.
This biting burning ache is not the gift I wish to pass down.
I step out of line to grieve this now;
so I don't have to watch my children grow burls around it. Atrophy.

Any child of mine riding in my sacred womb
doesn't need to imprint this lineage of suffering
a battered recipe, redacted, the only parts left outlining
how not to die.

Instead, I want them to receive the whole book we've penned together,
all our different shades of ink, on how,
how *gloriously,* to thrive.

I stand in the saltwater waist deep, and I am crying
the waves racking my body,
but between each surge I can still feel the dense silt
of the shore beneath me.

I am real.

The boat knocking against me as it rocks on the tide
the purpose of this poison I have chosen to imbibe
I volunteered; though terrified,
swirling on this, my generational tide.

Let me end this, grieve this, god-
dess   let me be soft enough, substantial

and staunch enough
able to turn and walk into the raw, rotting teeth /
face the breath of this

all of it
until it's   *felt enough* to   let go.

I watch my own body move in the water
but it's my mother's familiar blue veins that appear on *my* hands
as she picks up her suitcase and latches my front door,
waves once as she drives away from me, away from me
and my four-day-old son
like it's the easiest thing she's ever done before.

It's Mary's grief—though the exact sound is lost to me through time
as I wail over my own daughter
born too soon to have a body
but she still has a name—*Jade*—
the grief moves through me,
out my mouth, but I know it's also my grandmother's wail
that escapes me

lands softly in the boat.

And I'm breaking / picked apart at the seams / I'm a thousand
different me's
familiar and unseen
I can feel them / us / we
standing shoulder to shoulder behind me
passing me their *precious shards of grief.*

It's a chorus. A song. The wet sounds of us together.
A warm lament, hands reaching,
fingers entwined across time
as night falls, together we sing this pungent prayer.

//

In the quiet as the round moon rises,
an orca whale surfaces near the free floating boat.
Her black fin slaps the water,
her young calf there beside her.

I don't remember who lights the arrow
but it's burning
and I am pulling back.

I am the one with a body now, aiming

I let it go.

The arrow hits the boat. The fire igniting
as if our grief were gasoline.
A funeral pyre with buildings of white smoke.

The orca mother spouts her plume of water
forty feet up into the air,
and my breath catches
for a moment, I can't tell what is her plume of white sea water

and what is our smoke.

The Final Battlefield

I remember / soft / the edges of myself
              giving

all consuming / thin /   the light /   the heat,

shattering   glacial   heart

      baptised   in tears

in warming   water.

throbbing   bleeding

     feral   motherhood.

I   can   do   this.

I   can

        I   do   this;

give my own   breath
     to my own   child
self

       even thousands
          of miles away.

Epilogue

Little Gods

I am the crossroads.
My body growing a baby. A soft calcium self forming solidly
inside me while my hands work in the white sink, washing
the blood from my mother's black jacket.

I am home visiting, and her blood is everywhere. Dried and rusty
on my mother's plastic water jugs—which I refill— splattered
across the top of her gray Crocs; little speckles on the cement floor
of the bathroom. Her blood is everywhere—like Christ—except
there is no sacrament; no taking of it, anointing of it, blessing in it.

But we each are little gods, aren't we?
My glorious body building new bones, lungs, neurons,
a nervous system both pera and sympathetic.

And so is my mother's glorious body.

She built me, my bones; my brothers.
Now her holy body is inflamed, swollen, breaking
down,
red skin taught around the   cancer
as it grows, a big thundering cumulus
cloud around her ear
and her skin bleeds freely as though   asking

finally

for something

she doesn't have to clean up.

Conduit

She comes
in the autumn.

A spark in the dark
of my womb.

My body so ready
to build her new bones, a home.

We have no electric ultrasound image
of her tiny, big-hearted body.

No blood test to tell me that she is
my daughter.

But I feel her sturdy—sweet as a lick of honey— and
so ready for *this world*

which is already splitting open
around us like a too-ripe peach.

I hold the arms of my heart   wide
and welcome her   all of her

home.

Acknowledgments

This book would not exist without the continued encouragement, passionate-harassment and love of my best friend Teya who held the belief for this book before I could. She also provided the photography I didn't take, found on this book. I love you so much babes.

To my mother Lucy, thank you for giving me your heartfelt blessing for this book to be born, despite its very raw contents. Thank you for letting me be there with you at the end.

I am so thankful for my Goddess Circle Women: Zoe, Kathleen, Casey, Erin, Kadi, Amber, Camille, and Barbora who have listened and loved me in real-time and endlessly encouraged me and the soul of this book into being every Wednesday night since March 2020.

I am so grateful to my husband, Benjamin, for his support and passionate belief in me, there's no one else I'd rather do this life with.

To my EMDR therapist Katy, who by some miracle is a lover of poetry, and took many notes in session that then later became poems; thank you.

To my stunning poet friend Katherine McClintic-Wise, your heart, availability and keen eye in editing and support have meant so much to me and to the creation of this book.

To Kiowa, thank you for your support and careful listening and for sharing your emotional heart for words with me.

Thank you to Erica and Daxson Publishing who took a chance on me and this book. I feel so lucky to be one of the voices you are lifting up.

Thank you to my astonishing poet-buddy Aspen Everett who offered such heartfelt encouragement to me in the process of putting this book together; and to our CLI teachers, Marissa Forbs and TA Cecily Stone and our entire Denver cohort who offered me such a haven of support and encouragement after working so long in the dark by myself. THANK YOU.

Credits:

"Yellow," first published by Eunoia Review. February 2025.

"Crumple," first published in We Are The West: Embers. April 2025.

"The Great American PayWall" and "Drop Off" were first published in Screaming At America: An Anthology of Disobedience in 2025.

"Red Spring Run Off" first published in Matriarch: Meditations on Motherhood in 2025

Publisher's Note

Daxson Publishing was created to help marginalized artists and their allies publish their work, so the world can hear their voice. The vision for this publishing house is to help people get their work out there, and not have them struggle finding their way through the publishing process. Everyone's voice deserves to be heard, and we are here to help. If you are interested in submitting a manuscript, email daxsonpublishing@gmail.com. Support our cause by buying books from daxsonpublishing.com.

www.ingramcontent.com/pod-product-compliance
Lightning Source LLC
Chambersburg PA
CBHW020402130626
46549CB00006B/2408